D1378483

KALEIDOSCOPE

The Governor

Suzanne LeVert

BENCHMARK BOOKS

MARSHALL CAVENDISH
NEW YORK

Benchmark Books
Marshall Cavendish
99 White Plains Rd.
Tarrytown, NY 10591
www.marshallcavendish.com

Library of Congress Cataloging-in-Publication Data

LeVert, Suzanne.
  The governor / Suzanne LeVert.
     v. cm. — (Kaleidoscope)
Includes bibliographical references and index.
Contents: Who can be governor — Where governors live — The job of
governor — Other state leaders — Governors face the future —
Contacting your governor.
  ISBN 0-7614-1593-9
  1. Governors—United States—Juvenile literature. [1. Governors.] I.
Title. II. Series: Kaleidoscope (Tarrytown, N.Y.)
JK2447.L49 2004   352.23'213'0973—dc21   2003001665

Photo research by Anne Burns Images

Cover photo: Corbis/Bettman

The photographs in this book are used with permission and through the courtesy of:
Corbis: 13; Reuters NewMedia Inc., title page, 10, 18; AFP, 6, 17, 34, (Paul Richards, 41); Philip Gould, 9; Joseph
Sohm, ChromoSohm, Inc., 21; Bettman, 25; JFPI Studios, 37; Ronnie Kaufman, 38. *Getty Images:* George Best, 5;
Spencer Platt, 22; Joe Jaszewski/Newsmakers, 26; Blake Sell/Reuters, 29; Bill Greenblatt/Liaison, 30; Reuters, 42.
Office of the Governor: 14. *AP/Wide World Photos:* Dave Paczak, 33.

Series design by Adam Mietlowski

Printed in Italy

6 5 4 3 2 1

Contents

Who Can Be Governor 4

Where Governors Live 20

The Job of Governor 23

Other State Leaders 28

Governors Face the Future 40

Contacting Your Governor 43

Glossary 44

Find Out More 46

Index 48

Who Can Be Governor

Every state has a **governor**. He or she is elected by the state's citizens to head the **executive branch** of the state government, or the branch that makes sure the laws are followed. The governor of the state has two main jobs. First of all, he or she is the state's leader, sharing with the people its goals and challenges. The governor helps to motivate the people of the state to work toward these goals.

The governor has many roles to play as the state's chief executive officer. ▶
Here, New York governor George Pataki greets workers near the site of the terrorist attacks on the World Trade Center in New York City.

The governor's other important job is to act as the state's manager. He or she works with the state **legislature**, or law-making body, to create laws. These laws affect every aspect of citizens' lives, including the taxes they pay, the highways they drive on, and the schools they attend. The governor must work for the good of all the state's citizens.

◀ *Members of the Florida legislature rise before the beginning of a session. The governor works closely with the state's officials to make laws that will benefit all.*

Not just anybody can be governor. All states have requirements for the job. First you must be a U.S. citizen. You also have to be a certain age before you can serve, and you must live in the state you wish to govern. To become governor in Louisiana, for instance, a person must be at least twenty-five years of age and have lived in Louisiana for at least the past five years.

The governor represents his or her state and makes decisions that will ▶ *affect the state's future. Here former Louisiana governor Edwin Edwards addresses the state's citizens.*

People from all different careers and backgrounds have been elected to the office. Most governors have studied political science, business, or history. Twenty-three of the governors in 2002 had law degrees, and two were doctors. Several governors had served in the military, and two had received bronze stars for military service.

◀ *Mitt Romney was elected governor of Massachusetts in 2002. Before becoming the leader of his state, he was in charge of running the 2002 winter Olympics in Salt Lake City, Utah.*

The first two female governors were elected in November 1924. To date, twenty-three women have served as governors. In 1872 Pinckney Benton Stewart Pinchback of Louisiana was the first African American to serve as governor. He served for one month after Governor Henry Warmoth was removed from office by the U.S. Congress. In 1990 L. Douglas Wilder of Virginia became the first African-American governor chosen in an election.

The son of a white planter and a freed slave, Pinckney Pinchback was the first African-American governor. He served the state of Louisiana for one month in 1872. ▶

George R. Ariyoshi of Hawaii was the first Asian American to become governor, when he took over the job in 1973. He was then elected as governor for three terms. More recently Gary Locke became the governor of Washington in 1996. He was elected to another term in 2000. Washington voters were pleased with the ways he improved the state's schools and economy.

Gary Locke, the nation's first Chinese-American governor, has served two terms in his home state of Washington.

15

In New Hampshire and Vermont the governor is in office for two years. In the rest of the states, he or she serves for four years per **term**. Most states have rules about how long or how many terms a governor can serve. Virginia does not allow governors to serve more than one term. In other states, governors cannot serve more than two terms in a row. In about ten states, the governor may serve as many terms as he or she can win. As of 2002, Michigan governor John Engler was one of the governors who had served the longest. He held the office for twelve years in a row.

Caring for the state's natural resources, including water from the Great Lakes, was one of Michigan governor John Engler's main goals during his years in office. ▶

Most governors have worked in politics before taking office. Some have served in their own state legislatures or in the U.S. Congress. After finishing their terms, many former governors choose to remain in political life. Seventeen governors from ten states and two governors of former U.S. territories have gone on to become president of the United States, some right after finishing their term as governor. Two recent U.S. presidents took that path. Arkansas's Bill Clinton served two terms as president from 1993 to 2001, and Texas's George W. Bush took over the position after his election in 2000.

◀ *Many U.S. presidents first served as governors, including George W. Bush, who was the governor of Texas from 1994 until he became president in 2001.*

Where Governors Live

All but six states offer their governors a place to live. Usually called the **governor's mansion**, it houses the governor and his or her family while the governor is in office. One of the oldest states in the country, Massachusetts, has never had an official home for its governors. Governors there have lived in private homes and held public functions at the State House or in large public reception halls.

Most states offer their governors homes to live in while they are in office. ▶
In Iowa, governors live in the Terrence Hill Mansion in Des Moines. It was built in 1869 by Chicago architect William Boyington.

The Job of Governor

The governor of the state works to see that the laws of the state and the nation are carried out. The people elect a certain governor partly because they like the programs and policies he or she hopes to enact, or make into law. Once in office, the governor must then try and put those programs into action.

◀ In most states, citizens vote to elect the governor every four years.

One of the governor's most important jobs is to prepare the state **budget**. In doing so, the governor describes the major programs that he or she is seeking money for. One of the governor's supporters in the legislature presents the budget and the programs to the legislature. The governor then works with members of the legislature to try to pass laws and meet the goals of the state.

Former New York governor Mario Cuomo talks with reporters after having a budget meeting with members of the state legislature. It can take days or even weeks to get a state's budget approved.

▶

Governors also act as **ambassadors** to other states, to the national government, and even to foreign governments. They try to interest companies in investing in their states' economies. They also hope to attract visitors and to increase tourism in their states.

Every year or two years, the governor is required to report to the people the current conditions of the state's government and economy. This **state of the state address,** as it is often called, also gives the governor a chance to explain his or her plans for the near future.

◀ *In most states, the governor addresses the citizens and the legislature about the economy and other important issues. Here, California governor Gray Davis gives the State Address on January 8, 2000.*

Other State Leaders

The governor does not work alone. Many officials help him or her run the state. They are either elected by the people or appointed by the governor. One of the most important of these officials is the **lieutenant governor**. The lieutenant governor helps the governor perform his or her daily tasks. Also, if the governor dies or cannot finish the term, the lieutenant governor takes over the office.

Kathleen Townsend Kennedy became the nation's first female lieutenant governor when she took office in Maryland in 1995. In 2002, she lost the race for the governor's office to Parris Glendening. ▶

Most states also elect a **secretary of state**. His or her duties may vary according to each state's laws. In most states, the secretary of state makes sure that elections are fair. Usually the secretary of state also handles important records that are kept by the state government. These documents include business records and lists of drivers' licenses and license plates the state issues.

◀ *The secretary of state is responsible for keeping important state documents. In 2001, Missouri secretary of state Matt Blunt announced that many of the state's records, some of them dating from the 1790s, would be available on the Internet.*

Most states have two officials from the executive branch who handle the state's money. The **comptroller**, or controller as he or she is often called, inspects the state's accounts and approves expenses. The **treasurer** receives and pays out the money that comes into the treasury from income tax, the national government, and other sources.

States spend some of their money on protecting the environment. Here, New York governor George Pataki (left) and Vermont governor Howard Dean (right) sign an agreement to protect the water in Lake Champlain, which borders both states.

The **attorney general** is another elected position in many states. He or she acts as the state's lawyer in cases that citizens bring against a state official or agency. He or she also makes sure that companies doing business in the state do not pollute the environment or cheat or harm the public.

◀ *The state attorney general makes sure citizens are safe and healthy. Washington's Christine Gregoire (right) was one of eight attorney generals who worked to try and stop cigarette companies from targeting young people. Their efforts were praised by former president Bill Clinton.*

Other leaders who aid the governor in running the state head their own departments. The head of the department of education, often called the superintendent of schools or the secretary of education, helps decide what students need to learn and makes sure that school buildings and grounds are safe. Most states spend more on education than on anything else.

Most states have a department of education that makes sure children are safe at school. ▶

The secretary of health and human resources usually runs programs that help people who may be in need, such as the elderly, the disabled, and the poor. Other important leaders of the state help build and repair state highways, operate state-run hospitals, oversee the care of state parks, and manage the state's natural resources such as timber, minerals, and oil.

◀ *Health care remains an important issue for state governments. The secretary of health and human services makes sure all the state's citizens, from the youngest to the oldest, are well cared for.*

Governors Face the Future

The National Governors Association is a group that includes all the nation's governors. It meets twice each year to discuss the challenges these leaders face. In 2002 the governors discussed how to help their economies, how to improve education, and how to manage the rising cost of health care. Another concern for state leaders was security. Following the terrorist attacks on September 11, 2001, governors are more concerned than ever about the safety of their cities and towns.

Meetings of the National Governors Association offer the states' governors the chance to discuss common issues and challenges. In 1999, former Minnesota governor Jesse Ventura and then-governor George W. Bush of Texas greeted reporters before the start of that year's meeting. ▶

Contacting Your Governor

Your governor works for you, your family, and your community. If a problem or challenge exists in your neighborhood or town, you should feel free to contact your governor and let him or her know about it. You can also ask your local librarian for help or try the Internet. Most states' governors' offices have Web sites. Write a letter. Get involved. Your governor needs to hear from people of all ages.

◀ *Do you know who the governor of your state is? He or she welcomes the chance to hear from the citizens of your state—including young people such as you. Here, former New Jersey governor Christine Todd Whitman greets the public after her re-election to office in 1997.*

Glossary

ambassador—A nation's official representative.

attorney general—A lawyer who handles legal matters for the state.

budget—A plan for paying for programs important to the state.

comptroller—The person who examines the state's accounts and approves money to be spent on programs.

executive branch—The part of state government that makes sure laws are followed.

governor—A state's highest official.

governor's mansion—The place where the governor and his or her family lives.

legislature—A state's law-making body.

lieutenant governor—A state official who is second in command to the governor.

secretary of state—A state official who often runs state elections and handles business matters for the state.

state of the state address—The governor's report to the citizens about the conditions of the state.

term—The length of time an elected official serves in office.

treasurer—The person who collects the state's money and pays its bills.

Find Out More

Books

Feinbert, Barbara Silberdick. *State Governments.* Danbury, CT: Franklin Watts, 1993.

Giesecke, Ernestine. *Local Government.* Portsmouth, NH: Heinemann, 2000.

———. *State Government.* Portsmouth, NH: Heinemann, 2000.

Santrey, Laurence. *State and Local Government.* New York: Troll, 1985.

Shuker-Haines, Frances. *Rights and Responsibilities: Using Your Freedom.* Austin, TX: Raintree/Steck-Vaughn, 1993.

Organizations and Online Sites

Government for Kids—State Government
http://www.govspot.com/state/

Great Government for Kids
http://www.cccoe.net/govern/

Learning about the Branches of Government
http://www.kidspoint.org/columns2.asp?column_id=358&column_type=homework

Also, many state government Web sites have a kids' page for the state's youngest citizens. Do a search for your state's official site or have your parents, teacher, or librarian help you.

Author's Bio

Suzanne LeVert is the author of many books for young readers on a host of different topics, including biographies of former Louisiana governor Huey Long and author Edgar Allan Poe. Most recently, she wrote four books in Benchmark Books' Kaleidoscope series on U.S. government, *The Congress, The Constitution, The President,* and *The Supreme Court.*

Index

Page numbers for illustrations are in **boldface**.

ambassadors, 27
Ariyoshi, George R., 15
attorney general, **34**, 35

budget, 24
Blunt, Matt, **30**
Bush, George W., **18**, 19, **41**

citizens, 4, 7, 8, **22**, 23
Clinton, Bill, 19, **34**
comptroller, 32
Congress, U.S., 12, 19
Cuomo, Mario, **25**

Davis, Gray, **26**
Dean, Howard, **33**
department heads, 36-39

economy, 15, 27, 32, 40
Edwards, Edwin, **9**

Engler, John, 16, **17**
environment, **33**, 35
executive branch, 4, 32

governors,
    African-American, 12, **13**
    Asian-American, **14**, 15
    backgrounds of, 11
    female, 12, **42**
    jobs of, 4-7, 23-27
    mansions of, 20, **21**
    requirements to be, 8
    terms of, 16

health, **34**, **38**, 39, 40

Kennedy, Kathleen T., **29**

laws, 4, 7, 23, 24, 31
legislature, **6**, 7, 19, 24
lieutenant governor, 28, **29**
Locke, Gary, **14**, 15

National Governors

Association, 40, **41**
Pataki, George, **4**, **33**
Pinchback, Pinckney, 12, **13**
president, U.S., **18**, 19, **34**, **41**
programs, 23, 24

Romney, Mitt, **10**

secretary of state, **30**, 31
schools, 7, 15, 36, **37**, 40
state of the state address, **26**, 27

taxes, 7, 32
term, 16, 19
treasurer, 32

Ventura, Jesse, **41**

Whitman, Christine T., **42**